The World's Best Jewish Jokes

D1585537

Ben Eliezer

The World's Best Jewish Jokes

Illustrations by Menachem Gueffen

Fontana

An Imprint of HarperCollinsPublishers

Fontana
An Imprint of HarperCollins*Publishers*,
77–85 Fulham Palace Road,
Hammersmith, London W6 8JB

Published by Fontana 1992
9 8 7 6 5 4 3 2 1

First published in Great Britain by
Angus & Robertson (UK) 1984

Text copyright © Ben Eliezer 1984
Illustrations copyright © Menachem Gueffen 1984

The Author asserts the moral right to
be identified as the author of this work

ISBN 0 00637832 3

Set in 12 pt Goudy Old Style Bold
by Setrite Typesetters

Printed in Great Britain by
BPCC Hazells Ltd

Introduction

People have been telling jokes about their neighbours for millennia. They don't tell jokes about distant folk. Jokes about your neighbours help you to live with them. Most British jokes start, "An Englishman, an Irishman and a Scot..." because Britain is a union of these peoples. The French tell jokes about the Belgians, the Belgians about the Dutch, the Dutch about the Germans, the Germans about the East Friesians...and 2000 years ago the ancient Athenians told jokes about the Boetians.

Jews have been everyone's neighbours for a couple of thousand years, so there are a lot of Jewish jokes. Most Jewish jokes are told by Jews and very few Jews that I know mind when they're told by non-Jews. I mean, while they're telling jokes about us they can't be throwing stones at us! You can always tell a native Jewish joke from a joke told about Jews (and Jews enjoy both sorts). The former are unmistakable, but difficult to define. They revel in an insane logic, they almost always occur in unpleasant or disastrous circumstances and they're very funny. The latter are like all other neighbour jokes, which mock stupidity, laziness, meanness and all other characteristics common to our neighbours but remarkably absent from ourselves.

I had terrific fun writing this book and I want to thank all the friends who, on being told of my plans, racked their brains for Jewish jokes. To all those whom I brusquely interrupted with, "I've already got that one!" I apologise.

To James and Rebecca Hazeldine, Lew Rosenbluth, Mike Abrams, Bernard Henry, Menachem Gueffen, Paula Litzky, Jack Silver, Wendy Henry and many others, my warmest thanks, and especially to Richard who first asked me: "Do you know any Jewish jokes?"

Ben Eliezer
February 1984

D id you hear about the Jewish kamikaze pilot? He crashed his plane in a scrap-metal yard.

A t the funeral service for a very rich Jew, one of the mourners is beating his breast and wailing much louder than all the others. The rabbi, very concerned, taps him on the shoulder.

"I'm so sorry for you. No doubt you're one of the relations?"

"No! No!" sobbed the man. "That's why I'm crying!"

A Jew from London's East End goes to visit his son in Manchester. He shares his sleeping compartment with a non-Jew. As they are preparing for bed, the Jew says: "Excuse me. I wonder if I could borrow your towel? I seem to have left mine at home."

The man lends him his towel.

A little later the Jew asks: "Excuse me, but do you think I could borrow your vest? I seem to have forgotten my pyjamas."

Very surprised, the man lends him his vest.

A little later the Jew asks again: "I'm sorry to bother you, but I have forgotten my toothbrush. Could I borrow yours?"

The non-Jew could take no more. "No! That really is too much. I won't lend you my toothbrush!"

The next morning the son meets his father at the station. "Well, Father? Did you have a good trip?"

"Fine. But was I sharing with an anti-Semite!"

An Israeli soldier guarding a large number of Egyptian prisoners in the Sinai desert just after the Six Day War, told them: "Well, there's good news and bad news. Which do you want to hear first?"

An Egyptian corporal replied: "Let's hear the bad news first."

"Well, the bad news is, all we've got to eat is camel shit."

"Okay," said the Egyptian, "let's have the good news."

"There's plenty of it!"

When Marilyn Monroe was given her first matzo ball, she said, "Mmm! Delicious! Can you eat any other part of the animal?"

An air raid warning sounds in Tel Aviv, and as they rush into the air raid shelter one man says to another: "Oy vey! I've forgotten my false teeth!"

The second man shrugs: "So what do you think they'll be dropping? Sandwiches?"

What's the difference between a vulture and a Jewish mother-in-law?
A vulture waits until you're dead.

Two Jewish mothers met in the street.
"Well, Ruthie, how are the kids?"
"To tell you the truth, my Abie has married a slut! She doesn't get out of bed until 11, she's out all day spending his money on God knows what, and when he gets home, exhausted, does she have a nice hot dinner for him? Psha! She makes him take her out to dinner at an expensive restaurant."
"And Esther?"
"Ah! Esther has married a saint. He brings her breakfast in bed, he gives her enough money to buy all she needs, and in the evening he takes her out to dinner at a smart restaurant."

P resident John F. Kennedy was riding in a motorcade over Brooklyn Bridge in New York. "Pierre," he barked, turning to his press secretary, "why don't we stop somewhere small for a nice kosher pastrami sandwich on rye bread?"

"Good idea, Mr President. Just happens I know somewhere nearby in Brooklyn."

The motorcade sped off in a screech of tyres and drew to a halt outside Joe Cohen's sandwich bar.

Joe was sweeping the floor and swatting the flies; there were no customers. He looked up and rubbed his eyes in disbelief as eight huge, black Cadillacs drew up outside. And when the President got out and came into his bar, flanked by aides and secret service men, he thought he was seeing visions.

"Oy! Your Highness, Your Holiness, vot can I do for you?"

"Just a few dozen pastrami on rye with lots of mustard, please."

Joe slaved away, praying that one of his regular customers would come in and see the President in his shop. No-one came in.

"Now what do I owe you, Mr...er...er...Cohen?" asked JFK when Joe delivered the sandwiches.

"You? Owe me? Nutting, Mr President, nutting at all. Vos my pleasure entirely!"

"That's very kind of you, but I must do something."

"Vell, yes, you could. Come back here same time next week."

At the same time the following week the great motorcade drew up outside Joe Cohen's sandwich bar. This time the scene inside was quite different. The place was jammed. People were crawling on top of each other, contorted faces pressed to the window — Joe and his family were slicing meat, slapping on mustard, taking money for all they were worth. The President forced his way in.

"Well, Joe, here I am!"

"Jack! Jack!" said Joe, waving his finger, "I said not when there's business!"

T wo Jews meet on a train. One asks the other if he has the time. No answer. Again he asks. Again no answer. Eventually he taps him hard on the knee and almost shouts his question. And the other at last tells him the time.

"And why did it take you so long, if I may ask?"

"Well, it's like this. We'll get talking, we'll become friendly, when we get to Vienna I'll ask you to come home with me, have a bite to eat. And you'll meet my daughter, she's beautiful, and you're a nice-looking chap, and you'll fall in love and you'll want to get married. And quite frankly, I don't want a son-in-law who hasn't got a watch!"

What does an American Jewish Princess make for lunch?
Reservations.

Mrs Cohen arrived at Mrs Levy's house for a cup of coffee.

"My God, what flowers!" exclaimed Mrs Levy. "Where did you get such a wonderful bouquet?"

"Ech! It's nothing. I get one like this every week of the year."

"So who sends it to you? Do you have a lover?"

"You're crazy! My husband gives them to me!"

"And what do you have to do for them?"

"Do for them? I have to spend my life on my back with my legs in the air."

"Why? You've got no vase?"

How do you know when an American Jewish Princess has had an orgasm?
She drops her nail file.

A Jew, in Peking on business, finds himself alone on Friday night and, after many enquiries, eventually finds the local synagogue. He puts on his *talit* (prayer shawl) and begins to pray, surrounded by Chinese all doing the same. After the service, the Chinese rabbi goes up to him and asks him politely what he is doing there.

"Well, naturally, I like to go to synagogue on a Friday night."

"You Jew?" asks the rabbi.

"Of course!"

"You no look like Jew!"

Sitting next to well-known socialite Ruthie Plotnik at a gala ball, a newcomer to the glittering scene couldn't take his eyes off the magnificent diamond she was wearing. He couldn't restrain himself, he had to comment on it.

"Sure, it's wonderful," she agreed. "It's the Plotnik diamond."

"It's truly amazing. Tell me about it."

"Well," she replied, "unfortunately it has a curse attached to it."

"A curse!" he exclaimed. "What curse?"

"Mr Plotnik."

A rabbi finds himself sharing a rail compartment with a Roman Catholic priest. After some time, the priest leans forward. "Excuse me, Rabbi, but is it true that men of your faith may not eat pork?"

"Yes, Father, you're right," replies the rabbi.

"And tell me, between priests, confidentially, have you ever tasted it?"

"Well, as a matter of fact, a long time ago I did taste some bacon."

"And did you like it?" asks the priest.

"Yes, I must admit, I did."

A little while later, the rabbi leans forward. "Excuse me, Father, but is it true that priests are not allowed to have sexual intercourse with a woman?"

"Yes, Rabbi," the priest replies, "you're quite right, it's forbidden to us."

"And tell me, between priests, have you ever indulged?" asks the rabbi.

"Well, as it happens, no, I haven't."

"Mmm, pity," says the rabbi. "It's better than pork!"

While he was walking drunkenly down the street, an inebriated Jew bumped into a lamp post. "Anti-Semite!" he cursed under his breath.

An old Jew is run over by a car. He is laid gently by the side of the road. Someone fetches a blanket, and someone else gets a cushion to put under his head.

"Tell me, are you comfortable?" a woman asks.

"Ah well," he replies, "I make a living."

Father O'Malley called on his good friend Rabbi Goldbloom, in a highly agitated state. "Rabbi!" he gasps. "You've got to help me. I've got confession starting in 10 minutes and in an hour I've got to be miles away at a funeral. Can you come and take confession for me?"

"What, me? Take confession?"

"Sure, it's a piece of cake. Come down to the church — I'll start it off and then you can take over. You'll get the hang of it in no time."

When they got to the church the priest sat in the confessional, while the rabbi sat in a secret compartment within earshot. A woman came in. "Father, I have sinned."

"What have you done, my child?"

"I have committed adultery."

"How many times?"

"Four times, Father, and I sincerely repent."

"Put $2 in the box, say 10 Hail Mary's, and you'll be absolved."

Then another woman came in. "Father, I have sinned."

"What have you done, my child?"

"I made love to the lodger."

"How many times?"

"Twice, Father."

"Put $1 in the box, say five Hail Mary's and you'll be absolved."

As soon as the woman had left, the priest whispered to the rabbi, "Okay, can you take over now? I must dash."

"Sure," replied the rabbi, "I've got the hang of it." The rabbi settled himself into the priest's position, well hidden. A woman came in. "Father," she said, "I have sinned."

"What have you done, my child?" asked the rabbi.

"I have committed fornication."

"How many times?"

"Just once, Father."

"Well, you'd better go and do it again."

"What! Do it again?"

"Sure, it's two for a buck."

Two Jewish businessmen meet in the street. "Well, Moishe, how was your fire?"

"Ssh!" hissed the other. "It's not till next week!"

An old Jewish woman was sharing a compartment on a train with a distinguished-looking young man who was reading *The Times*.

"Excuse me, young man, can I ask you something? Tell me, are you Jewish?"

"No. I'm not."

A little later: "Tell me, are you sure you're not Jewish?"

"Of course I'm not!" And he buried himself behind *The Times* in a rage.

A little later: "Excuse me, young man, are you really sure you're not Jewish?"

Utterly exasperated, he exploded. "All right, yes, I'm Jewish!" he said, to keep her quiet.

"Hmm. Funny, you don't look Jewish."

I n Morocco, a Jew and an Arab shared a farm, but times got hard and they decided they had to split up. But how to divide the assets was a problem: all they had left was a goat, a cow and a hen.

"I know," said the Arab. "You take the hen, and I'll take the goat and the cow."

The Jew refused.

"Okay then, you take the goat and I'll take the cow and the hen."

Still his Jewish partner refused.

"Okay," suggested the Arab, "let's eat the cow now, then I'll have the goat and you have the hen."

Still the Jew refused.

"I'll tell you what," said the Jew, "you have the goat, if you like, and the cow and I will take the hen."

B eckie and Solly Feigenbaum are in bed. "Listen, Beckie," says Solly, "do me a favour and close the window, it's cold outside."

"And if I close the window, will it be warm outside?"

Two disciples of a famous rabbi came to visit him and while they were waiting to be ushered into his presence, the rabbi's wife brought them two cups of lemon tea and a plate with two cakes on it, one small, the other big.

"After you," said one disciple to the other, offering him the plate.

"No, after you."

"No, no, I insist, after you."

"Na, you take first."

Eventually one of the two helped himself first — to the bigger cake. The other was outraged: "What! You helped yourself first and took the bigger cake!"

"So?" said the other. "And if you'd chosen first, which cake would you have taken?"

"Why, the smaller one of course!"

"Well, what are you complaining about? You've got the smaller one!"

Two Jews were on safari, in the middle of the jungle. As they were treading their way warily through the trees, all of a sudden a huge, snarling wild cat leapt down from a branch and sank its teeth into Solly's neck.

"Aaahhh!" Solly shrieked. "Hymie! What is it?"

"How should I know?" retorted Hymie. "You're the furrier!"

Two old friends met for the first time in many years.

"Morrie! How are you?"

"Fine, Bennie, and how's yourself?"

"Wonderful. Listen — mine Joe is getting married next Sunday and I want you should come."

"I'd love to."

"Wonderful. You know the Golders Green synagogue? Right, well you take the third turning on the left, the second on the right and third on the left again. You go to number 43 and you ring with your elbows."

"Ring with my elbows? Why?"

"Well, you're coming with presents aren't you?"

A Jew, riding on a bus in Moscow, sees an old friend of his running behind the bus, puffing and gasping. When the bus stops he asks him what he was doing.

"Easy, Moishe," puffed the friend, "I just saved three kopecks."

"Do me a favour, Yossel. Save yourself three roubles and run behind a taxi!"

A mother gave her son two ties for his birthday, a striped one and a spotted one. The next day he wore the spotted one. "So what's the matter with the striped one? You don't like it?"

A Jew goes into a kosher restaurant in New York and is served by a Chinese waiter speaking fluent Yiddish. "Tell me," he says to the owner when paying, "how come you've got a Chinese waiter that speaks Yiddish?"

"Ssh!" replies the other. "He thinks it's English."

An old Jew is run over in front of a church. A priest runs out and whispers in his ear, "Do you believe in the Father, the Son and the Holy Ghost?"

The Jew opens his eyes. "I'm dying, and he asks me riddles!"

Two Jews are in front of a firing squad. They are offered a blindfold. One refuses it, with a curse. The other says, "Ssh! Don't make trouble!"

The maths teacher points to the back of the class. "Abie," he asks, "what's four per cent?"

Abie shakes his head. "You're right," he replies, "what's four per cent?"

Solly Cohen took his beautiful secretary out to dinner. Afterwards, back at her apartment, he grew amorous, but no matter what they tried he couldn't achieve an erection. Eventually, full of apologies, he gave up trying and, shamefaced, went home. Sliding into bed next to his fat, snoring wife, her thigh touched his and he had an erection. Shaking his head in disgust, he got out of bed, looked at his erect organ and said, "Now I know why they call you a shmock!"

A rabbi and a priest are locked in fierce theological disagreement.

"Of course making love is work, and not pleasure," said the priest. "It's God's work, in fulfilment of His Law."

"No, no," said the rabbi, "it's a pleasure. If it weren't, the human race wouldn't have survived."

They agreed to consult their superiors and meet again. A month later they met.

"Well, it's settled," said the priest. "The Archbishop and the Cardinal all agree, it's work."

"No," said the rabbi, "the Chief Rabbi agrees with me. It stands to reason, if it was work we'd make the maid do it!"

A man asked a rabbi why God had created gentiles. "Well," came the answer, "someone's got to buy retail."

And then there was the Jewish Santa Claus. He came down the chimney and said: "Hi, kids! You want to buy some presents?"

I t's Easter and a priest is getting cost estimates for the church flower arrangements. A Catholic florist says £300.

"Much too much," says the priest, "but the florist is one of the flock."

A Protestant florist offers to do the arrangements for £250.

"Cheaper," thinks the priest, "but he's not of the flock and the difference isn't that great."

While he is pondering, Solly Goldberg gives him a price of £75! That settles it. Solly gets the contract.

On Easter morning, the flock file into a church filled with magnificent azaleas, camellias, carnations and roses and above the altar, spelt out in daffodils, the Easter message: "Christ is risen! But Goldberg's prices never vary."

An old Jewish woman was sharing a train compartment with a smart young man. Every few minutes the old lady shook her head and sighed, "Oy! Am I thirsty!" And again, "Oy veh, am I thirsty!"

Eventually, utterly exasperated, the young man leapt to his feet, flung himself down the corridor and returned with a cup of water. "Here, drink that!" And he thrust it into the old lady's grateful hands. He settled back in his seat and picked up his book again.

Then, another groan from the old lady: "Oy! Was I thirsty!"

Two smart ladies meet in the street.

"Beckie, you're looking wonderful! What have you been up to?"

"Well, Molly, guess what! I'm having an affair."

"An affair! Wonderful! Tell me, who's doing the catering?"

Morrie Feigenbaum had been saving for a cruise all his life. Eventually the time came when he could afford it and he booked for a splendid Caribbean cruise. His wife accompanied him down to the New York docks and waved goodbye as he went up the gangplank.

The minute Morrie entered the ship, rough hands grabbed him, stripped him of his clothes and thrust him down rotten stairs into a huge cavernous area in the depths of the ship. The light was dim and the air fetid. Amid harsh, confusing shouts he was shackled to a plank and a rough oar was thrust into his hands. Then came the sound of drums and in stalked a huge, hairless brown man with an enormous drum. Men marched up and down with whips, crying, "Row, you scum. Row!" Next to him on the bench was a white-haired skeleton of a man, who could scarcely pull his oar. All the time the huge bald man beat his drum, and Morrie tried desperately to row in time.

After many days they reached Jamaica, but Morrie and all the other oarsmen stayed chained to their benches, and when again the drum began they had to row all the way back to New York.

Eventually, after many more days of exhausting rowing to the beat of the drum, they arrived back at Manhattan docks.

As they tied up, Morrie turned to the old, white-haired man next to him — it was the first time they had spoken — and said, "Listen, I've never been on a cruise before. Please, tell me how much I should tip the drummer."

"Well," replied the ancient, "I gave him $10 when I did the same cruise last year."

There was a very long queue outside the pearly gates, everybody waiting their turn patiently. Then a short man, muttering and sighing loudly to himself, just barged by all the other people and pushed his way through the gates. People protested loudly at this rude behaviour. Someone asked St Peter who it was. "Oh, that was God. He's fine most of the time, but sometimes he thinks he's a doctor."

Hymie Cohen and his friend Mick Murphy have adjacent shops in London's East End. After five years Hymie owns the whole block, while Mick still only has a small stall.

"Hymie, I'm fed up. We both work the same, tell me, what's the secret of Jewish business success?"

"Easy," replies Hymie. "Gefillte fish."

"Gefillte fish? Well you'd better let me have some."

Hymie sells Mick a pound for £5. On his way home Mick notices another stall selling gefillte fish for only £2.50 per pound. He returns to Hymie's. "Listen, Hymie, it's very kind of you to give me the secret of Jewish business success, but I saw gefillte fish on sale down the road at only half the price."

"See," said Hymie, "it's working already!"

Abie was on his death bed. "Sarah," he croaked, "are you there?"

"Yes, Abie, I'm here."

Silence...then: "Morrie, are you there?"

"Yes, Abie, beloved brother, I'm here."

Silence, but for Abie's agonised breathing..."Wilbur, are you there?"

"Yes, Dad, I'm here."

Silence..."Milton, are you there?"

"Yes, Pop, I'm here."

Abie jerked himself up, and shouted, "So who's minding the shop?"

A man left his shoes for repair at a Jewish cobbler's, but before he could collect them the war broke out and he didn't get back to the shop for five years. He returned with the ticket.

"You may not remember them, but they were dark brown brogues with light brown laces."

"Sure I remember," said the cobbler. "Come back next Tuesday, they'll be ready."

A very orthodox rabbi died and went to heaven. He was astonished to find himself at a dinner table sitting between Abraham and Moses, and all round were famous sages, teachers and saints. An angel came by to serve him some food and the rabbi asked, "Excuse me, but who's doing the catering?"

"Why," the angel replied, "it is Most High God himself."

"I see," answered the rabbi. "In that case I'll take the fish."

A schools survey showed there was no crime among Jewish pupils. An inspector asked a Jewish schoolboy what he thought was the reason for this. "Easy," came the reply. "Crime doesn't pay."

Goldberg meets Ginsberg at the station.

"Tell me, Ginsberg, we meet here every day, and often at the synagogue and the golf club. And you never ask me how's business."

"Okay," replies Ginsberg. "Tell me, Goldberg, how's business?"

"Ach," replied Goldberg, "don't ask!"

Why were the Ten Commandments written on two separate tablets?

Well, God offered them first to the Germans. "Impossible!" they replied. "What's this stuff about thou shalt not kill? It's natural to kill!" And they refused.

So then God offered them to the French. "What's this rubbish about thou shalt not commit adultery?" they exclaimed. "It's in our blood! It's *l'amour!*" And they refused too.

So eventually God offered them to the Jews.

"How much are they?" asked the Jews.

"They're free," came the reply.

"In that case we'll take two!"

Goldberg and Ginsberg competed for luxuries. One day Ginsberg called Goldberg on the phone. "Hello there, Goldberg! Guess where I'm calling from?"

"Okay. So tell me!"

"I'm calling from the car!"

Goldberg turned green with envy. He worked like crazy for a year, saving every penny. Eventually he called Ginsberg's car from his car: "Hi, Ginsberg! Guess where I'm calling from?"

"Hold on, Goldberg! I'm on the other line!"

After making his flight information announcement the Israeli pilot on the El Al jet forgot to turn the intercom off and his next words were heard throughout the cabin. "I'll have a cup of coffee, then I'll screw that gorgeous new stewardess, Leah."

Leah was down the end of the passenger cabin and ran forward to tell the pilot to turn the intercom off. Halfway down, an old man tripped her up. "Can't you wait, Leah? Let him have his coffee first."

A Jew owns a remarkable parrot — it can *daven* (pray in Hebrew). He decides to take it to the synagogue and make some money. After the service he gathers 20 or so acquaintances round him. "This parrot," he announces, "can *daven*."

"Psha! Piffle!" they all cry.

"Okay, so we'll take a bet."

Odds of 25 to one against are agreed, the money is laid on the table.

"Okay, go ahead!" he instructs the parrot. The parrot does not move. "Go on, *daven!*" Nothing. He cajoles and begs the parrot to *daven* but to no avail. He pays out a fortune.

When he gets the parrot home he is about to strangle it, when the bird says, "Wait! Wait! See what odds you get next week!"

An Israeli tried to smuggle two huge sacks of coffee (a high tax item in Israel) past customs at Tel Aviv.

"It's bird food," he protested, when caught.

"Oh yes? Birds don't eat coffee!" replied the customs officer.

"Look," the man replied, "if they like it they'll eat it, if they don't they won't!"

During the Six Day War some officers went to see Moshe Dayan, well known for his collection of antiquities. "We've got good news and bad news. The good news is that we've got the Pyramids. The bad news is that they won't fit in your garden."

Two partners in the rag trade decide that times are so bad one of them must commit suicide to preserve the business. They toss coins and Morrie goes to the window to jump from their 24th storey showroom. They shake hands one last time and Morrie leaps out. As he sails past the window of a competitor on the 17th floor, he shouts back up to his partner, "Izzy! Lace cuffs next season!"

Two Jewish commandos are deep inside the Libyan desert waiting to ambush Colonel Gaddafi. Says one: "Okay. Let's go through the schedule once more. At 8.55 the advance guard come by and we kill them with the mines; at 9.05 the bodyguard arrive and we kill them with machine guns; then we grab Gaddafi and tie him down in the sand and smear him with honey; at 9.15 the rearguard approach and we call in an air strike to deal with them. Everything clear?"

"Yeah, sure, but it's 9.10 already. I hope nothing's happened to him!"

Why do Jews have big noses?
Well, air is free!

Two middle-aged Jews who were once at school together meet in the street, outside the Savoy Hotel. One is expensively dressed and has just stepped from a Rolls Royce; the other is a shabby beggar. The beggar accosts the rich man. "Hey, Abie, remember me? It's Solly, your old friend! Do me a favour, give me £5 for a bed."

"Sure! Sure," replied the other, putting his arm round him. "Bring it round in the morning and I'll take a look at it!"

An Israeli arrived in Paris, went to a brothel, asked for a whore by name and gave her £150 for her services. The next night he returned. Again he asked for her and again gave her £150. The third night also he gave her £150.

"Listen," she said, after the third time, "tomorrow night if you come back you can have it for nothing. I really like you."

"Actually," he replied, "I have to return to Israel tomorrow. Besides, I know your brother there. He gave me £450 to give to you."

On a kibbutz in Israel a young bull said to an old bull, "Let's run down the hill and screw some of the cows."

"Na," said the old bull, "let's walk down the hill and screw all the cows."

A Jew in a restaurant asked the waiter, "Oy! Do you have matzo balls?"

The waiter replied, "No, I always walk like this."

A Catholic priest, an Anglican parson and a rabbi were walking through the back streets of their parish after an ecumenical meeting. They were horrified to see through lit and uncurtained windows a couple making love. After a careful look, the priest declared that the offending pair were most certainly not of his flock.

"How do you know?" asked the others.

"Simple, there's no crucifix on the wall."

The parson also took a look and declared smugly that they were not of his flock either.

"How do you know?" asked the others.

"There's no Bible on the shelf," he replied.

It was the rabbi's turn to look in, and he returned with a look of shame. "I'm afraid they're from my congregation," he declared.

"How do you know?" asked the others.

"Fitted carpets," replied the rabbi.

Mr and Mrs Goldberg went on a skiing holiday to Switzerland. On the first day, Goldberg told his wife he was going off skiing all day in the high mountains. "Don't worry, Beckie, I'll be back by five, or six at the latest."

She waited nervously all day, and when he hadn't returned by seven she begged for a search party to be sent out. Eventually a Red Cross rescue team — a full complement of guides, St Bernard dogs and army mountaineers — set off. They climbed to the high slopes, calling as they went, "Mr Goldberg! Mr Goldberg! It's the Red Cross! Where are you?" No reply. Up they went to the high valleys. "Mr Goldberg! It's the Red Cross!" No answer still. Eventually, almost at the glacier, they called out once more, "Mr Goldberg! It's the Red Cross!"

And a faint answer came back: "I've given already!"

Why don't people make love on the pavement in Israel?

Because passers-by would point out what they were doing wrong.

A very religious rabbi died and his adoring followers prayed to God to have just a glimpse of him in heaven. Their wish was granted, but, to their horror, they saw him with a beautiful blonde on his lap.

"Rabbi! Rabbi!" they cried. "How can you behave like this, you, who were always so saintly?"

"Listen, you don't understand," replied the rabbi. "She's not my reward. I'm her punishment!"

A farmer in his fields was astonished to see a small green thing with antennae coming out of its head and flashing lights for eyes.

"Where do you come from?" he asked.

"The planet Mars," came the reply.

"And tell me, are all the inhabitants of Mars green?"

"Sure."

"And do they all have stalks coming out of their heads?"

"Yes."

"And do you all have three blue legs?"

"Of course."

"And do you all have so many rings on your hands and necklaces around your necks?"

"Oh no. Only the Jews."

Mrs Ginsberg has been trying to become a member of an ultra-smart golf club and when her husband dies and leaves her a lot of money she changes her name to Lonsdale-Gordon, has elocution lessons, takes lessons in etiquette, has a nose job and eventually becomes a member. For her first dinner there she wears a splendid gown. A passing waiter, however, pours a plate of soup over her. Horrified, she stands up and yells: "Oy veh!" and, looking around her, adds, "whatever that may mean."

One of the aides to the Israeli Prime Minister rushed into his office.

"Prime Minister! A catastrophe!"

"What? What?" asked the Prime Minister.

"A drought."

"Where?"

"In the Negev."

"Oh! Thank God. You had me worried for a moment. I thought it was in America!"

A schnorrer (a Jewish beggar) knocks loudly on the front door of a millionaire's apartment at two o'clock in the morning. No answer. He knocks again. Still no answer. He keeps knocking, until after half an hour the angry millionaire comes down and opens his door.

"Can I have sixpence, please?" asks the schnorrer.

"What do you think you're doing waking me up in the middle of the night, just for sixpence!"

"Listen," replies the schnorrer, "do me a favour. I won't tell you how to run your business, don't you tell me how to run mine!"

A Jew asks an orthodox rabbi to say a *brocha* (a blessing) over his new Ferrari.
"What's a Ferrari?" asks the rabbi, and refuses.
So the man asks a reformed rabbi.
"What's a *brocha*?" asks the rabbi.

Moses and Jesus play golf. Moses tees off with a superb 250-yard drive. Then Jesus drives off and as the ball soars in the air it's caught in the beak of a passing eagle who's flying in the direction of the green. He drops it into the pouch of a squirrel on the ground who runs to the flag and pops it into the hole. Moses turns to Jesus: "Look," he asks, "do you want to play golf or do you want to mess around?"

A Jew is sitting on a train opposite a priest.

"Tell me, er, Your Worship," the Jew says, "why do you wear your collar back-to-front?"

"Because I'm a father," answers the priest.

"I'm also a father and I don't wear my collar like that."

"Ah," said the priest, "but I'm a father to thousands."

"Then maybe it's your trousers you should wear back-to-front!"

Two chauffeurs are waiting for their bosses to emerge from evening prayers at the synagogue. While they are lounging by their Rolls Royces, the sound of a trumpet is heard from within.

"Hey! What's that noise?" asks one.

"Why, they're blowing the *shofar*."

"Hey! They sure are good to the staff!"

At a barmitzvah celebration at London's luxurious Dorchester Hotel the guests were delivered individually in 500 white Rolls Royces. The cabaret featured Frank Sinatra and Leonard Bernstein with the Vienna Philharmonic. The food was smoked salmon and the drink Dom Perignon. Then the guests were all flown first class to Kenya where they set out on safari on elephant back. An hour or so out, they all halted. The guests grew restless. "What's the hold-up?" one asked.

The answer came back: "There's another barmitzvah up ahead."

In Russia, before the revolution, a powerful local police chief lost his favourite ring. He offered an unlimited reward. Eventually a local Jew found the ring and the police chief, true to his promise, offered the Jew anything he wanted.

"Well, Jew, what do you want?"

The Jew replied: "All I want is that you should forget I exist."

One Friday evening, in a little Jewish town in Poland, a stranger who arrived at the synagogue for the Sabbath service was invited home to stay with a well-to-do member of the congregation. They ate well, studied a little *Talmud*, discussed the affairs of the world and at the end of the Sabbath the stranger was presented with a bill by his host. He was astonished.

"What!" he exclaimed. "You would charge me for your hospitality on the Sabbath?"

"Of course," replied the other.

"I've never heard of this before!"

"Quite normal, I assure you. Do you want to check with our rabbi?"

Off they went, and the stranger was appalled to hear that the rabbi agreed with his host. So he handed over the 500 zlotys and left for the station.

As he was waiting for his train to leave, his host arrived and returned the money to him.

"But why all this nonsense about demanding the money, checking with the rabbi and then coming to the station to return it to me?"

"Well," replied his host, "I just wanted to show you what an idiot we had for a rabbi!"

Two children were playing with their dog by the sea when the dog was carried out by a big wave. A passing rabbi dived in, saved the dog and revived it by artificial respiration. The children asked, "Hey, Rabbi, are you a vet?"

"Am I vet?" replied the rabbi. "I'm soaking!"

A Jew and a non-Jew shared a compartment on a train. Time after time, as they pulled out of each station, the Jew shook his head and moaned "Oy, oy, oy! Oy, oy, oy!"

Eventually the non-Jew, exasperated, asked him what the matter was.

"Oy, oy, oy! Am I on the wrong train!"

A Catholic priest, an Anglican parson and a rabbi were discussing how they divided the money that they collected between the poor of their parish (God's share), and themselves.

The priest said: "I draw a square on the ground, throw the money into the air and what lands in the square is mine; the rest is God's share."

The parson said: "I draw a circle on the ground, throw the money in the air and what lands inside the circle is mine; the rest is for the poor."

The rabbi said: "It's simple. I throw all the money in the air and what God wants, he keeps. Anything that falls to the ground, I keep."

A man walking down Fifth Avenue in New York asks a Jew where Minsky's bagel shop is. The Jew is carrying parcels, and hands them over to the other man to hold. Then he spreads his hands out wide and shrugs. "How should I know?" he asks.

A Jewish doctor gave a patient six months to live. But when the man didn't pay he gave him another six months.

During the German occupation of Warsaw an officer of the SS was patrolling a poor street when he came across an old Jew sitting in the street against a wall. "Jew, one of my eyes is glass. Which one?" he asks.

"That one, the left one," answered the Jew.

"How do you know?" asked the Nazi officer.

"It's the more human one."

A Jew is having a drink at the bar of a hotel when an oriental gentleman accidentally knocks over his drink.

"You damned Japanese!" yells the Jew. "First you gave us Pearl Harbour, now this!"

"Hold on a minute. I'm not Japanese, I'm Chinese."

"Chinese, Japanese — so what's in a name?"

"And you Jews," replies the Chinese, "you can talk! You sank the *Titanic*!"

"We sank what?" asked the astonished Jew. "The *Titanic* was sunk by an iceberg!"

"Iceberg, Goldberg. So what's in a name?"

Moses and Jesus came back to earth and went to Galilee to meet their respective supporters. They competed in performing miracles and went to the water's edge to walk on the water. Moses went first and did it perfectly. Then Jesus tried, but he sank to his waist immediately. As Moses was hauling him out he whispered in his ear, "On the stones! On the stones!"

How do we know Jesus was Jewish? Simple. He lived at home till he was 30; he went into his father's business; his mother thought he was God and he thought she was a virgin.

Hymie Goldberg, an ultra-religious Jew from Brooklyn, decides to visit his old friend in London. It's the hottest day of the year as the QE2 docks at Southampton and Hymie comes down the gangplank dressed in his full-length gaberdine coat, his broad-brimmed fur-trimmed hat, his prayer shawl and his heavy boots. As he nears the dockside, the dockers can no longer restrain their laughter. Hymie stops at the bottom, looks around and says: "What's the matter with these people? Have they never seen an American before?"

A Jew comes home one night and finds out that his wife has been unfaithful. He tells a friend that he's going to kill her.

"Don't do that," says the friend. "If you kill her you'll go to gaol and be hanged. You should screw her to death!"

So the Jew makes love to his wife day and night for a year. His friend comes round to visit him and is shocked to find him a haggard and shaking old man. But his wife looks wonderful, shining with health.

"How is it you're so ill and she's so well?" asks the friend.

"Ssh! Don't say anything! She doesn't know she's dying."

Mr Cohen comes home one night and starts to pack his bags.

"So where are you going?" asks his wife.

"To Tahiti."

"Tahiti? Why Tahiti?"

"Simple. Every time you make love there they give you $5."

Then Mrs Cohen starts packing her bags.

"So where are you going?" asks Mr Cohen.

"I'm going to Tahiti."

"Why?"

"I want to see how you're going to live on $10 a year."

A KGB agent comes across a Jew reading a Hebrew grammar book on a bench in Gorky Park. "Hey, Jew," he says, "why are you bothering to read that? You know we'll never let you go to Israel."

"Well," says the Jew, "I'm reading it in case they speak Hebrew in heaven."

"And what if you go to hell?"

"Ah," sighs the Jew, "Russian I already know."

Myra tells Isaac that she wants a divorce. "I've got another lover," she announces.

"Never," says Isaac, "never! I don't believe in divorce. But listen, if your lover's a nice man bring him home to live with us."

So the lover goes to live with them, and eventually Myra becomes pregnant. One day they're all out for a walk in the park and Isaac runs into an old friend.

"You look so well," says the friend. "Tell me, who's the nice young woman?"

"That's my wife."

"And who's the young boy?"

"That's my son," answers Isaac.

"And who's the nice-looking young man over there?"

"Ah!" says Isaac, "that's my schmock."

One Israeli to another: "What we should do is declare war on America."

"What? You're crazy. They'd destroy us."

"Sure they would, then they'd give us lots of money for reconstruction. Who knows — they'd probably make us the 51st state."

"Okay," replied the other, "but what happens if we win?"

Ginsberg goes to Goldberg's shop to buy a cupboard.

"We don't sell cupboards," says Goldberg, "we sell clocks. Here, buy a nice clock." And he lifts up from under the counter a very ornate gold clock.

"Na," says Ginsberg, "who needs a clock? I don't need a clock."

"You don't need a clock? Of course you need a clock. Tell me, wise man, how do you know when to get up in the morning?"

"Ach! Easy. The man next-door turns his radio on at seven o'clock exactly. I can hear the announcer."

"So how do you know when to go to work or when to come home?"

"By the time I get out of bed and have a wash and a shave, it's half past seven. By the time I've had a boiled egg and toast it's a quarter to eight, time to leave for the office. By the time I get to the bus stop it's ten past and the bus comes in a few minutes and by the time it gets to my stop it's half past eight which is when I start work.

The factory siren next-door sounds at 12 and by the time I have lunch and walk round the block it's one o'clock, time to start work again. At five o'clock another siren goes and by the time I get home on the bus it's half past five and I have a rest. By the time I make something to eat and watch a bit of television it's time to go to bed and the next thing I know the man next-door is playing his radio and it's time to get up. So tell me, Goldberg, why do I need a clock?"

"So what happens if you wake up in the middle of the night and you want to know what time it is?"

"Easy! I've got a trumpet."

"You've got a trumpet? How do you tell the time with a trumpet?"

"I go out on the balcony and blow as hard as I can."

"And how does that tell you the time?"

"Psha! The anti-Semite that lives opposite opens his window and yells out: 'Hey! you mad Jew! What are you doing playing the trumpet at three o'clock in the morning!' "

A group of Jewish women decided to improve their intellectual level. No more talk of maids or children or sons-in-law — but only politics and social questions: Poland, El Salvador, Afghanistan, the Bomb.

Then one said: "And what about Red China?"

"I love it! I love it!" said Sarah. "Especially on a nice, white tablecloth."

Many years ago, in Poland, long before the establishment of the state of Israel, a fervent Zionist sent out a wedding invitation: "The service will be held on Temple Mount, Jerusalem, at 11 a.m. on Sunday, 4th November." At the bottom of the invitation in tiny letters, these words also appeared: "If, on the other hand, the Messiah has not yet come, then the service will be at The Akiva Synagogue, Casimir Street, Warsaw."

An Englishman, an Irishman and a Jew were each sentenced to 20 lashes. The judge asked each of them what sort of oil or ointment they wanted on their backs as protection.

"I'll have some olive oil, please," said the Englishman, and received his lashes.

The Irishman said, "I'll have nothing on my back! I'm strong, and I despise British justice!"

Then the Jew was asked what he wanted on his back. "The Irishman," he said.

I t's Abie and Rachel's wedding anniversary. Abie buys her a magnificent fur coat. On the way back from the furrier Rachel says, "Abie, take the second left turning, please."

"Why?" asks Abie. "That's not the way home."

"Look, Abie, for once in your life just do as I ask without arguing. Now take the third turning on the right. Good, now stop here on the left. You see that office building? That's yours, all yours. It's my present to you."

"Rachel! This whole building? I don't believe it. It's impossible."

"Here are the deeds, Abie. It's all yours."

"How on earth did you pay for it?"

"Well," Rachel replies, "you know every time we make love you give me $10? Well, I've saved it all and invested it."

"My God!" exclaims Abie. "If only I'd known, I'd have given you all my business."

M oses arrives at the Red Sea with the Israelites, the Pharaoh and his army in hot pursuit. He calls his public relations officer, Morrie, over in a rage.

"Where are the boats?"

"Boats? Who said anything about boats?"

"I must have boats to cross the water! What do you want me to do, part the sea and walk through it?"

"Hey, Moses, if you do that," says Morrie, "I'll get you two whole pages in the Old Testament!"

A rabbi was staying at a luxury hotel. At midnight there came a knock on his door, and, bleary eyed, he opened it.

"Hello there," said a ravishing blonde in a clinging evening gown. "Are you Frank Sinatra?"

"No, miss," replied the rabbi, "I'm Rabbi Greenspan from Arndale Heights, New Jersey." He returned to bed, but an hour and a half later the doorbell rang again.

"Hi, there, are you Frank Sinatra?" asked an exquisite redhead.

"No," said the rabbi, "I'm Rabbi Morris Greenspan." He returned to bed.

About an hour later there was another knock on the door. This time it was a tall, raven-haired beauty wearing only high heels, black stockings and a tiny pair of panties.

"Are you Frank Sinatra?"

"Am I Frank Sinatra?" echoed the rabbi, and he threw his arms out and sang at the top of his voice: "Strangers in the night...two lonely people... strangers in the night..."

A schnorrer stops Mrs Feigenbaum in the street. "Oy vey, lady. I'm weak from hunger. I haven't eaten in four days!"

"So," she says, "force yourself!"

S olly has been tossing and turning all night long, unable to sleep.

"Solly, what's the matter?" asks Beckie.

"It's that £500 I owe Benny. I have to repay him tomorrow and I haven't got it."

Beckie opens the window wide and yells at the house opposite: "Benny! Benny! You know that £500 Solly owes you? He's due to pay you back tomorrow, right? Well, he hasn't got it!" She shuts the window and says, "Now let him do the worrying — you go to sleep."

A n old Jewish lady is crossing the street when a car races round the corner, knocks her over and comes screeching to a stop.

"Hey, watch where you're going, can't you!" shouts the driver.

"Why?" the old lady shouts back, as she struggles to her feet. "Are you coming back?"

W hen Groucho Marx was told that he was not allowed to swim at the country club because he was Jewish, he asked, "And what about my son — he's only half Jewish, can he go in up to his waist?"

A beautiful woman consults Dr Greenberg, the psychologist, as she has been having hallucinations. "Get undressed will you, please?" he asks. She does as she is told and the doctor makes her lie down and then makes love to her. "Well," says the doctor, "that takes care of my problems, now let's hear about yours."

S olly and Molly are driving along in the Rolls Royce, and while they're at a red light a beautiful blonde taps at the window. Solly opens the window.

"Hello, Solly, how are you? Long time no see. I've got some wonderful new lingerie, why don't you come around some time?"

"Okay," Solly says. "I'll see you tonight at eight o'clock."

"Solly!" says Molly. "Who's that?"

"That's my mistress. And before you complain think of the six mink coats I've got you and the apartment in Miami. Do you want to come to the Savoy for tea?"

While they're having tea Molly points someone out to Solly on the other side of the room: "Hey, Solly! Who's that with Joe Cohen? It's certainly not Beckie Cohen."

"That's Joe's mistress," answers Solly.

"Psha!" says Molly. "She's not as nice as our mistress!"

After he had designed a new industrial process of great benefit to the Soviet Union, a Jewish engineer was asked what he wanted as a reward.

"A phone call to my brother in New York," said the Jew to the local commissar.

"You know that's impossible, think of something else: a holiday by the Black Sea, a sable coat for your wife, a dacha in the country..."

But the Jew would not be persuaded.

His request gradually filtered up the party hierarchy until it landed on the desk of the great Stalin himself. Stalin agreed, on two conditions: that the phone conversation be held in his office and that it be limited to one word. Eventually the Jewish engineer was ushered into the Great Leader's office, and he picked up the phone and dialled his brother in New York.

"Remember," said the Father of the People, "only one word."

He eventually got through, and as his brother answered the phone, the Jew screamed: "*Help!*"

The KGB knocks on Yossel Finklestein's door one night. Yossel opens the door.

The KGB man barks out, "Does Yossel Finklestein live here?"

"No," replies Yossel, standing there in his frayed pyjamas.

"No? So what's your name then?"

"Yossel Finklestein."

The KGB man knocks him to the ground and says: "Didn't you just say you didn't live here?"

"You call *this* living?"

A 16-year-old student at a *Yeshiva* (religious university) tells his father, "I have these urges all the time."

His father tells him to go and see his rabbi, which the youth does.

"Rabbi," the student says, "even in the middle of studying I get an erection."

"Pray harder," advises the rabbi.

"Well?" asks the boy's father on his son's return.

"I've prayed as hard as I can but I still get urges."

"Well, go and see the rabbi again."

He went, but the rabbi was out, and so the rabbi's wife asked him in and wanted to know what his trouble was.

"I get these terribly strong urges," he says.

"Ah, come with me," she says, and takes him up to the bedroom and makes love to him.

"So?" asks the father when his son gets home. "What happened?"

"It was wonderful," says the boy. "The rabbi's wife's got more brains between her legs than the rabbi has in his head!"

What's the difference between an American Jewish Princess and a barracuda?
Nail polish.

An Englishman, an Irishman, a Frenchman and a Jew are all in a plane that's about to crash. "Let's make a pact," they say. "Whoever survives will put £200 in the others' graves to speed them on their way to the next world and to thank God for surviving."

The plane crashes and the Englishman is killed. The others go to his funeral, and, as agreed, the Irishman puts £200 in notes into the Englishman's grave. The Frenchman also solemnly contributes his £200. The Jew writes out a cheque for £600 to the Englishman, puts it in the grave and takes the £400 change.

The local fire brigade has a brand new fire engine and they decide to ask the local religious leaders to give it their blessing. The priest sprinkles it with holy water and chants a few words in Latin. The parson waves a cross at it and chants, "And may the Good Lord bless all who ride in her." The rabbi just wanders over to the engine and cuts two inches off the hose.

Hymie to his lawyer: "I'll hire you if you're positive you can win the case."
Lawyer: "Tell me the story."
Hymie launches into a terrible tale of fraud and cheating in his business.
Lawyer: "It's an open and shut case."
Hymie: "Oh God! That's terrible!"
Lawyer: "Why's that?"
Hymie: "I just told you my partner's side of the story!"

A Jewish groom was working in the Tsar's stables. One day the Crown Prince came in and called to him: "Moishe, get together the very finest carriage you can. The Princess is coming home, I just had a telegram. The best harness with plumes, you know."

As Moishe was getting things ready he noticed that one of the horses had an erection. "Hey!" said Moishe to the horse, "who had the telegram, you or the Prince?"

All the Israelis living in America decided to ask the President to grant them a separate state. Their wish was granted but negotiations broke down when they couldn't find anyone to be ambassador to Israel.

One Jewish doctor to another: "All day long I hear stories of pain and suffering. 'Doctor, my back!' 'Doctor, my stomach!' 'Doctor, my wife!' It's awful, I tell you. Tell me, Sam, how come you look so serene after a day listening to the world's troubles?"

Second doctor: "So who listens?"

Beckie says to Ruthie: "You look so good! What's your secret?"

"Well," says Ruthie, "the thing is, last Monday a handsome young boy knocks on my front door and asks, 'Is Hymie your husband in?' and when I say no, he picks me up, takes me upstairs, puts me on the bed and makes love to me for three hours. Tuesday, a knock on the door. Same boy. He asks if my husband is in and when I say no, he picks me up, carries me upstairs, throws me on the bed and makes love to me for four hours. Yesterday, same thing. Knocks on the door, asks if my Hymie is in, I say no, he picks me up, takes me upstairs, makes love to me for five hours. Only one thing puzzles me..."

"What's that?" asks Beckie.

"What does he want with my Hymie?"

T wo Jewish salesmen, bitter rivals, meet at the station.

"So where are you going?" asks one.

"I'm going to Tarnopol."

"Ha! When you tell me you're going to Tarnopol I know that you think that I'll think you're going to Zbarazh, but this time I know you're really going to Tarnopol, so why are you lying?"

T wo Jews arrive at the pearly gates of heaven and ask St Peter if they can come in. "Certainly not," says St Peter. "We don't allow your sort in here. Go on, scram!" He goes off and proudly tells Jesus what he's done. Jesus goes crazy.

"Peter," he says, "you can't do that. Quick, go and get them back."

Peter runs off and comes back, panting. "They've gone!" he says.

"Who?" asks Jesus. "The Jews?"

"No, the gates!"

Milly Levy says to Dr Ginsberg, her psychiatrist: "Kiss me!"

Ginsberg says: "That's all I need! I shouldn't even be lying next to you!"

A Jewish restaurant.

"Hey, there! Mr Waiter! What's with this chicken soup?"

"What do you mean what's with the chicken soup?"

"It tastes funny."

"So...laugh!"

"Oy vey! Rabbi Levy, it's a terrible business! Old Evie Ginsberg owes the moneylender £500 and she hasn't got two beans. They're going to throw her out of her apartment, she can't feed the children and she's got a bad back and can't work..."

"Terrible business," agrees the rabbi. "I'll raise some money at the synagogue right away. I'll give £50 myself and the Jewish Welfare board will give £100. Tell me, are you a relation? What's your connection?"

"Ech! Me? I'm the moneylender."

For 60 years Yetta lived with her dreadful husband, Moishe. He was mean, nasty and always drove her mad with his demands for kinky sex. One fine day Moishe died. Yetta had him cremated and took his ashes home in a box. With the box in her hand she walked around the house talking to the dead man.

"Moishe! Look at that fridge. All those years you wouldn't let me spend a shekel on food. Now look! It's full of steaks and champagne, bagels and smoked salmon. Moishe, now look in my wardrobe! All the time you were alive you never allowed me more than one new dress every two years. Now look! It's full of furs and silk dresses and the jewel box is full of diamonds. And Moishe, all those years you never let me have a say in the business, well, today I took over as chairman."

And she opened the box with his ashes in it as she finally said: "And as for that blow job you were always nagging me for — wwhhoosshh!"

A New York Jew goes to Los Angeles. He is sitting round the pool in Beverly Hills when he hears a great row going on at the other end.

"So what's going on?" he asks his Californian friend.

"It's a battle of wits," his friend replies.

"What, here in Hollywood? Who?"

"Liebowitz, Horowitz and Markowitz."

G insberg meets Goldberg.

"So how's your son, Lou the lawyer?"

"Fantastic! Every lawyer should do so well. He's so busy he can't take any new cases."

"And Sarah?"

"What a girl! She's just back from Europe — she's played the violin in every city, in the best concert halls."

"And how's your son Jeremy?"

"Ach! He's still selling schmutter (clothes) on the lower East side. Mind you, without him we'd all be starving."

Old Abie Cohen is on his deathbed. He calls his beloved wife. "Hetty! I'm going!"

"Oy, Abie! Don't leave me..."

"I've been thinking...I want to leave the business to Sammy."

"Na! Not Sammy, he's only interested in pleasure. Leave it to young Izzy..."

"Okay. The beach house I'll leave to Naomi..."

"Psha! She hates the sea. Leave it to Rachel."

"Okay. The diamonds I'll leave to Ruthie..."

"Na. She's a scruff. Leave them to Naomi."

"Okay. The Rolls Royce I'll leave to Izzy..."

"Rubbish! He can hardly drive. He's smashed up his last two cars. Leave it to Sammy."

"Listen, Hetty, can I ask you something?"

"Sure, Abie. What is it?"

"Tell me, who's dying?"

While on his church rounds Father O'Brien sees three children playing together — two small strangers and Michael O'Conner, one of his flock. He stops, is introduced and, thinking of priestly duties, tells the children he'll give $2 to whoever can answer the question, "Who was the greatest man on earth?".

The boys think for a minute and one of the strangers, Mark Bunyan, bursts out: "President Kennedy."

"Sure now," says the priest, "he was a good man all right, but not the greatest. Come now, Michael," he prompts, "you should know this if you remember your catechism."

"Well, Father," says Michael, "I'd say it was St Patrick because he brought Christianity to Ireland."

"No, Michael. It's a good answer, but not the right one," says the priest, and he confidently repockets the $2.

But Isaac Goldstein, the other stranger, pipes up: "It was Jesus Christ."

The priest pays up, but with a puzzled air. "Isaac," he asks, "surely someone of your faith doesn't believe that?"

"Oh no, Father. I know Moses was the greatest. But business is business."

S ammy meets Solly in the street.

"So? Why so glum?" asks Solly.

"Have I got problems! I've got to raise a million dollars in a week."

"So? Easy! Get a million candles and sell them for a dollar each."

"But I've got no candles."

"Then you've got problems."

A schnorrer stops a respectable-looking man in the street and asks for some money.

"I'm sorry," says the man, "but I never hand out money in the street."

"So what should I do?" asks the schnorrer, "open an office?"

After the Israelis conquered the old city of Jerusalem in 1967, they announced that they had done a deal with the Jordanians to share out the Wailing Wall between them. The Israelis would keep the wall — the Jordanians could have the wailing.

Solly visits Sam at his house and is surprised to see him scraping the paint off the walls and putting it into a paperbag. "Sammy!" exclaims Solly, "what are you doing? Are you redecorating?"

"Na," answers Sammy. "We're moving!"

S olly meets Morrie walking down the road.
"Morrie, what's up? You look as though the cares of the world are on your shoulders."

"Solly, the worst has happened. You know my son Lou, the best son a man ever had? He worked hard, passed all his exams to medical school. Became the best surgeon in this city. I sent him to Israel as a reward and what happens? He comes back a goy. I'm going to the rabbi to ask advice."

"Funny you should tell me this, Morrie, but you know my son Leon? A better son wasn't known of. Works hard, passes all his exams to law school. Graduates top of the class. Becomes the best lawyer in the country. To reward him I sent him to Israel. What happens? He comes back a goy. I'll come to the rabbi with you."

They go to the rabbi, tell their story and the rabbi says: "Oy vey! Do I know how you feel? Mine son Moishe, works hard, passes all his exams to become a rabbi. Becomes the best *Talmudist* in the country. As a prize I sent him to Israel and he comes back a goy!"

The three men decide to make a pilgrimage to Jerusalem to pray for God's guidance at the Wailing Wall. They arrive at the wall, and tell God their sad stories, when all of a sudden there's a clap of thunder and a terrible voice comes down from the sky: "You think you've got problems? I have this fine son called Jesus, he goes into the family business, I send him to Israel to be the Messiah, and you know what? He comes back a goy!"

Use the remaining pages for any favourite jokes not included in this book – then cut them out and send them to the publisher for Jewish Jokes 2.